Sleep Tight, Little Wolf

Qongchu', ngavyaw' mach

A picture book in two languages

Ulrich Renz · Barbara Brinkmann

Sleep Tight, Little Wolf

Qongchu', ngavyaw' mach

Translation:

Pete Savill (English)

Lieven L. Litaer (Klingon)

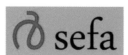

Download audiobook at:

www.sefa-bilingual.com/mp3

Password for free access:

English: **LWEN1423**

Klingon: **LWKLI2021**

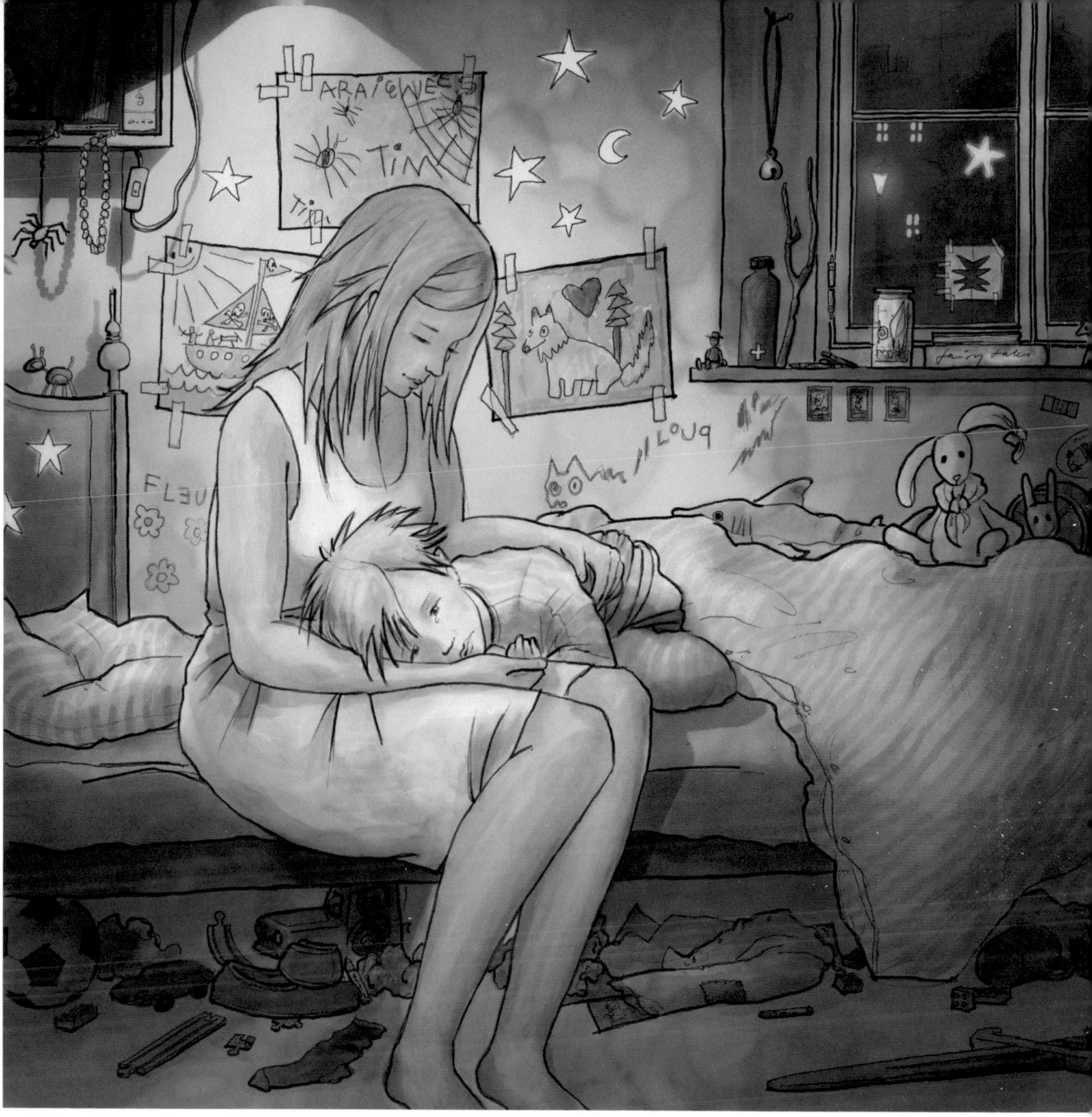
ARAIGNEE
TIM

Good night, Tim! We'll continue searching tomorrow.

Now sleep tight!

maj ram, tIm! wa'leS manejqa'.

DaH yIQongchu'!

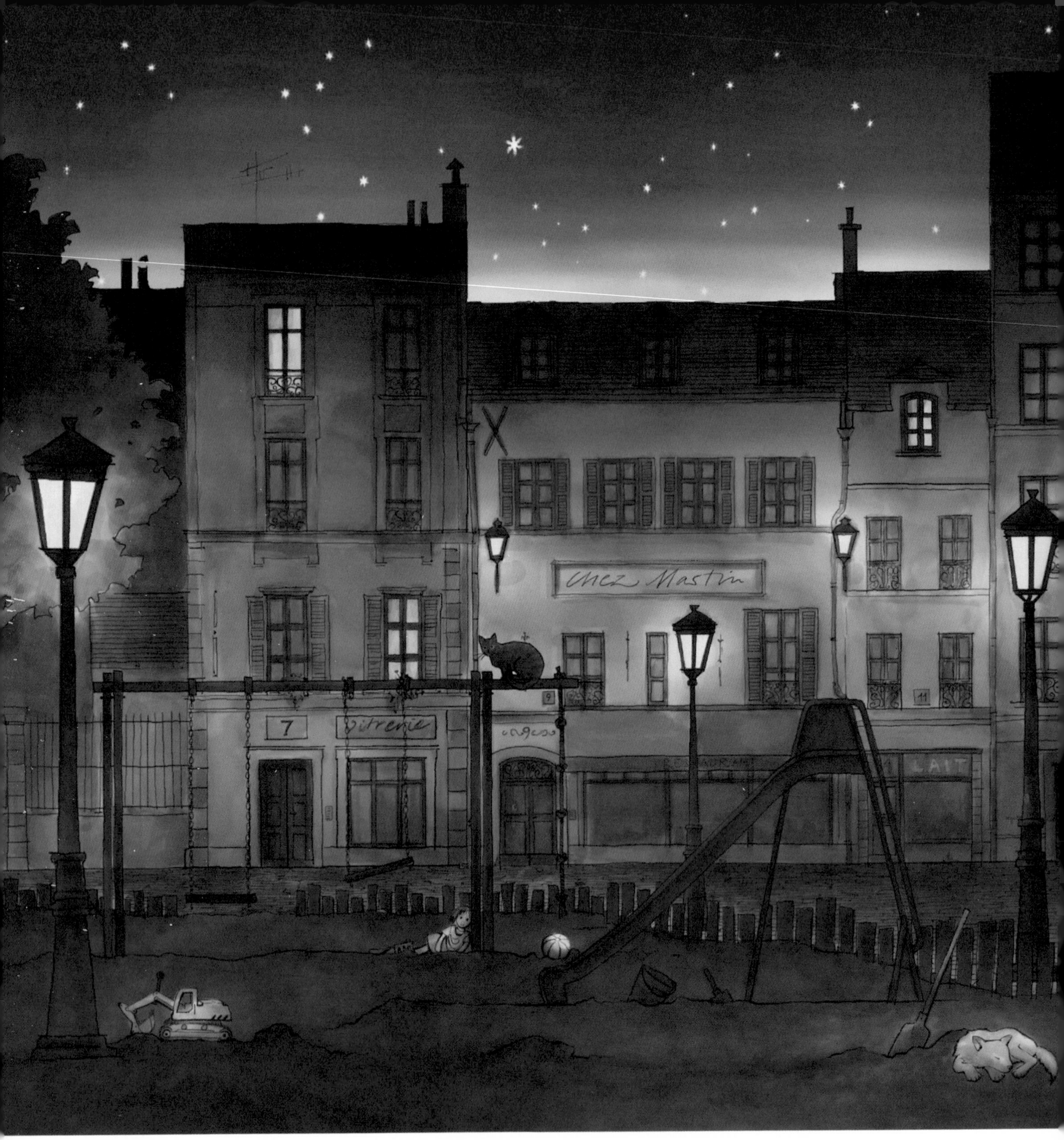
Chez Mastin
7
Vitrerie
LAIT

It is already dark outside.

HurghchoHpu' chal.

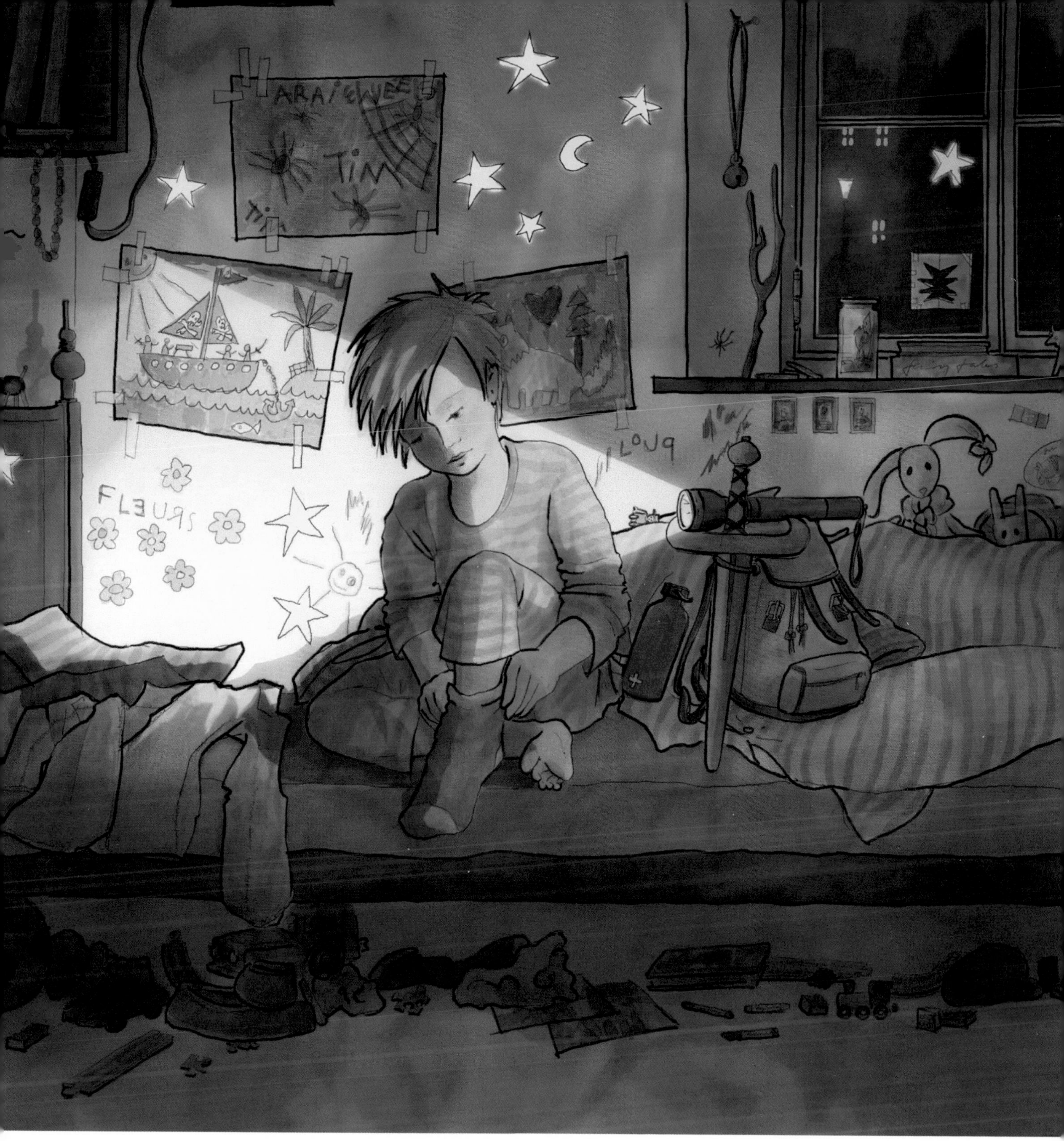
TIM

What is Tim doing?

nuq DIghtaH tIm?

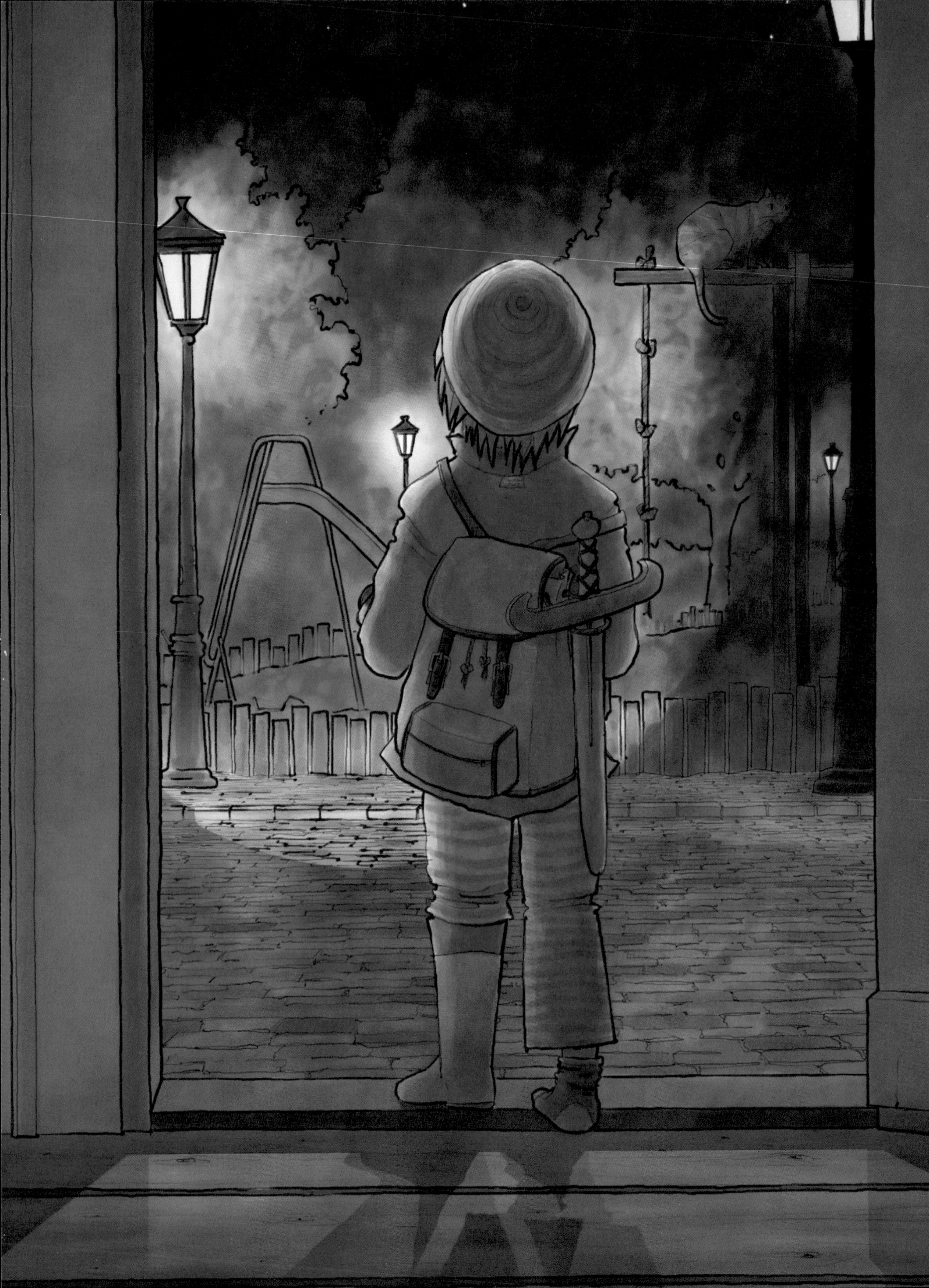

He is leaving for the playground.

What is he looking for there?

juHDaj mej, reHmeH Daq ghoS.

pa' nuq nej?

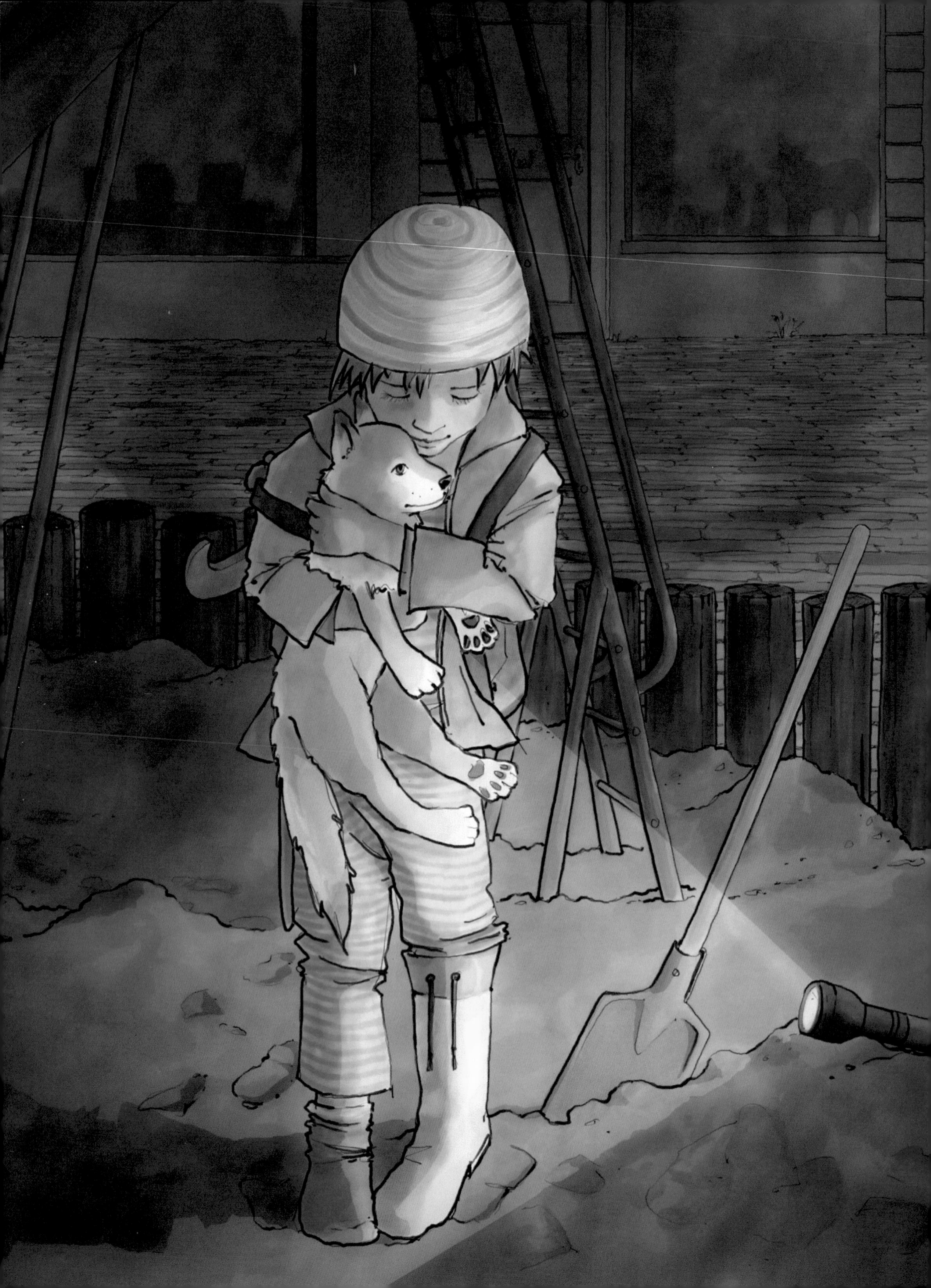

The little wolf!

He can't sleep without it.

ngavyaw' mach'e' nej.

'oH HutlhtaHvIS QonglaHbe' ghaH.

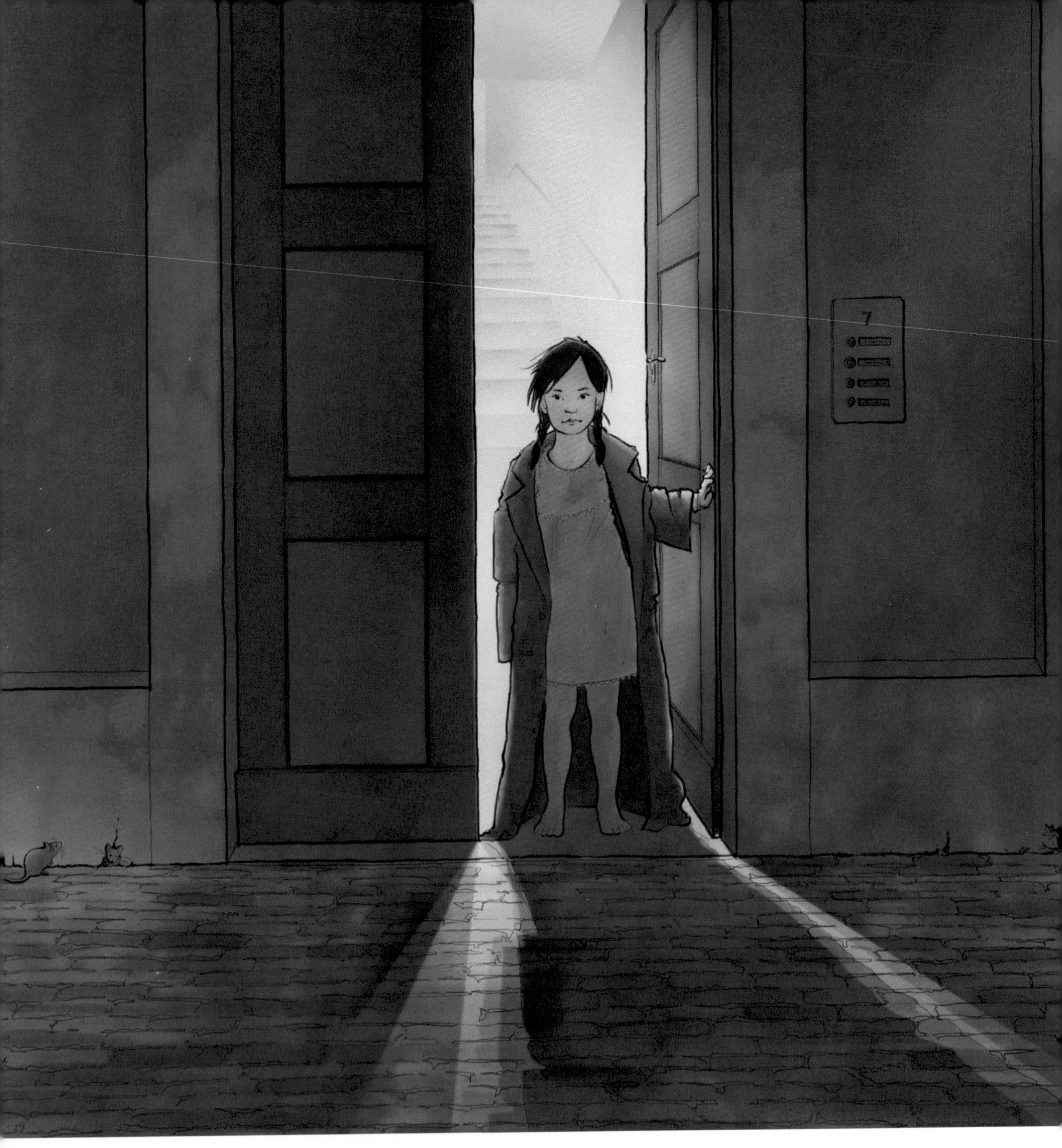

Who’s this coming?

toH. chol 'Iv?

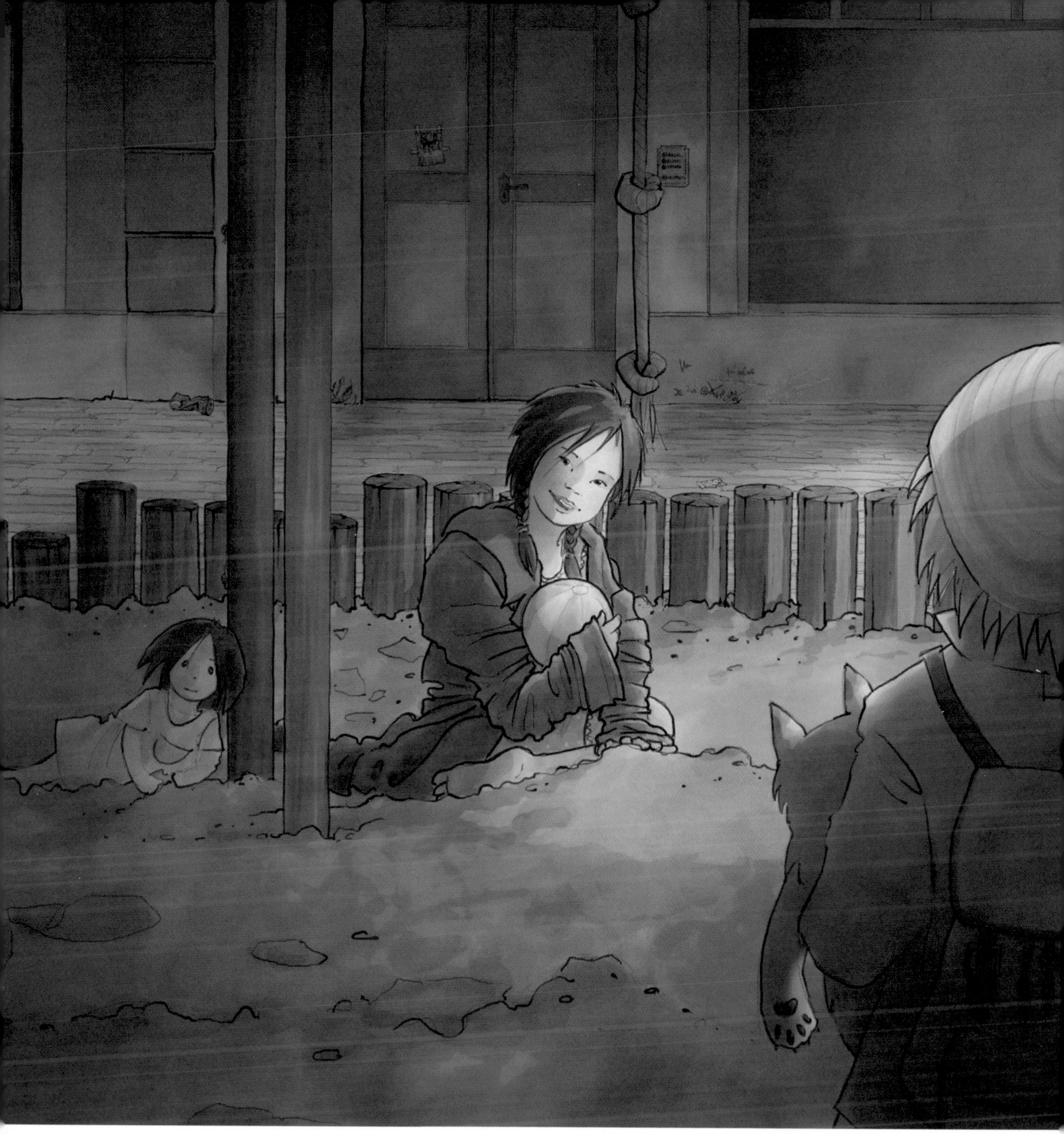

Marie! She’s looking for her ball.

marIy! QujmeH moQDaj nejba'.

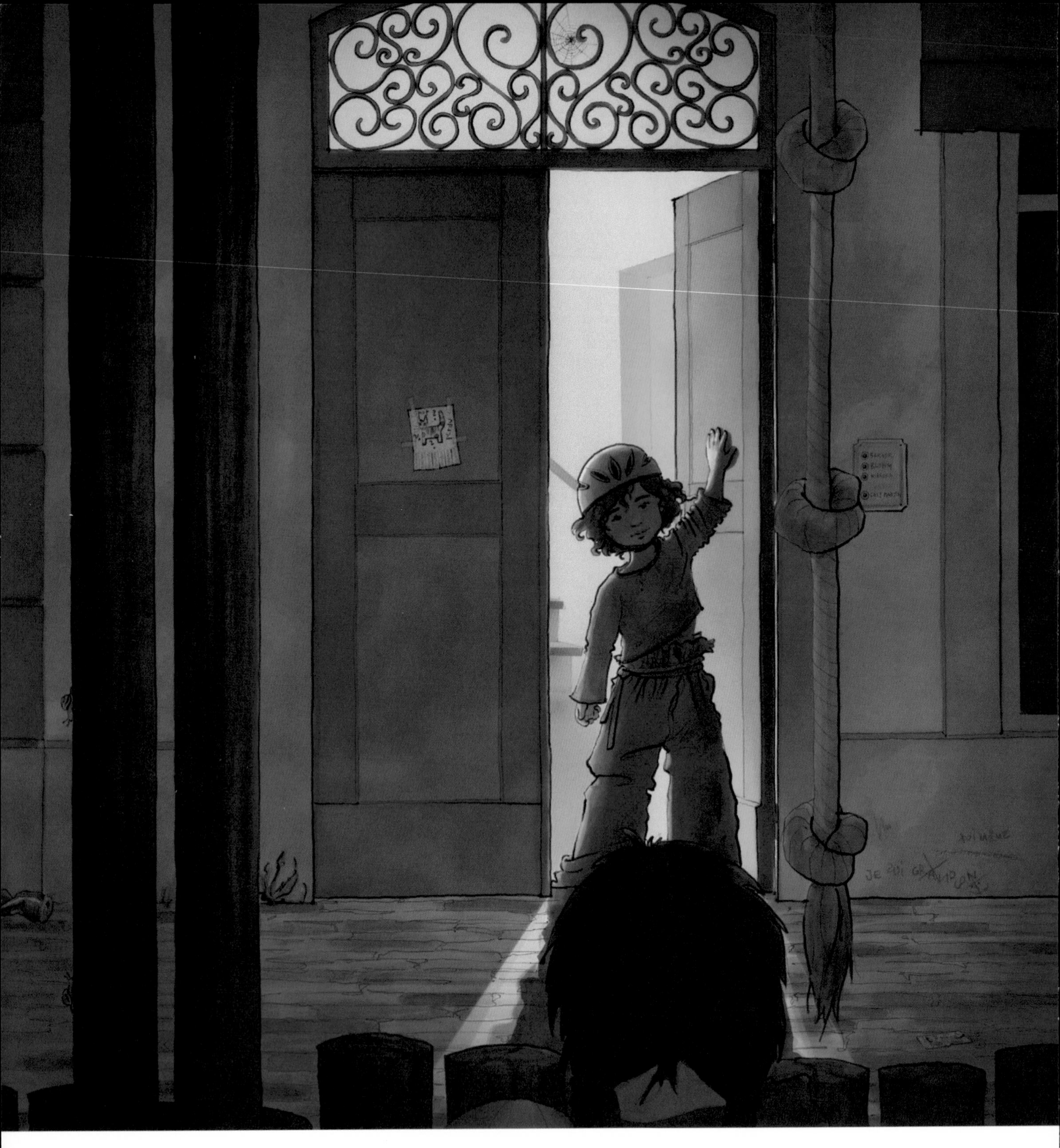

And what is Tobi looking for?

'ej nuq nej tobIy?

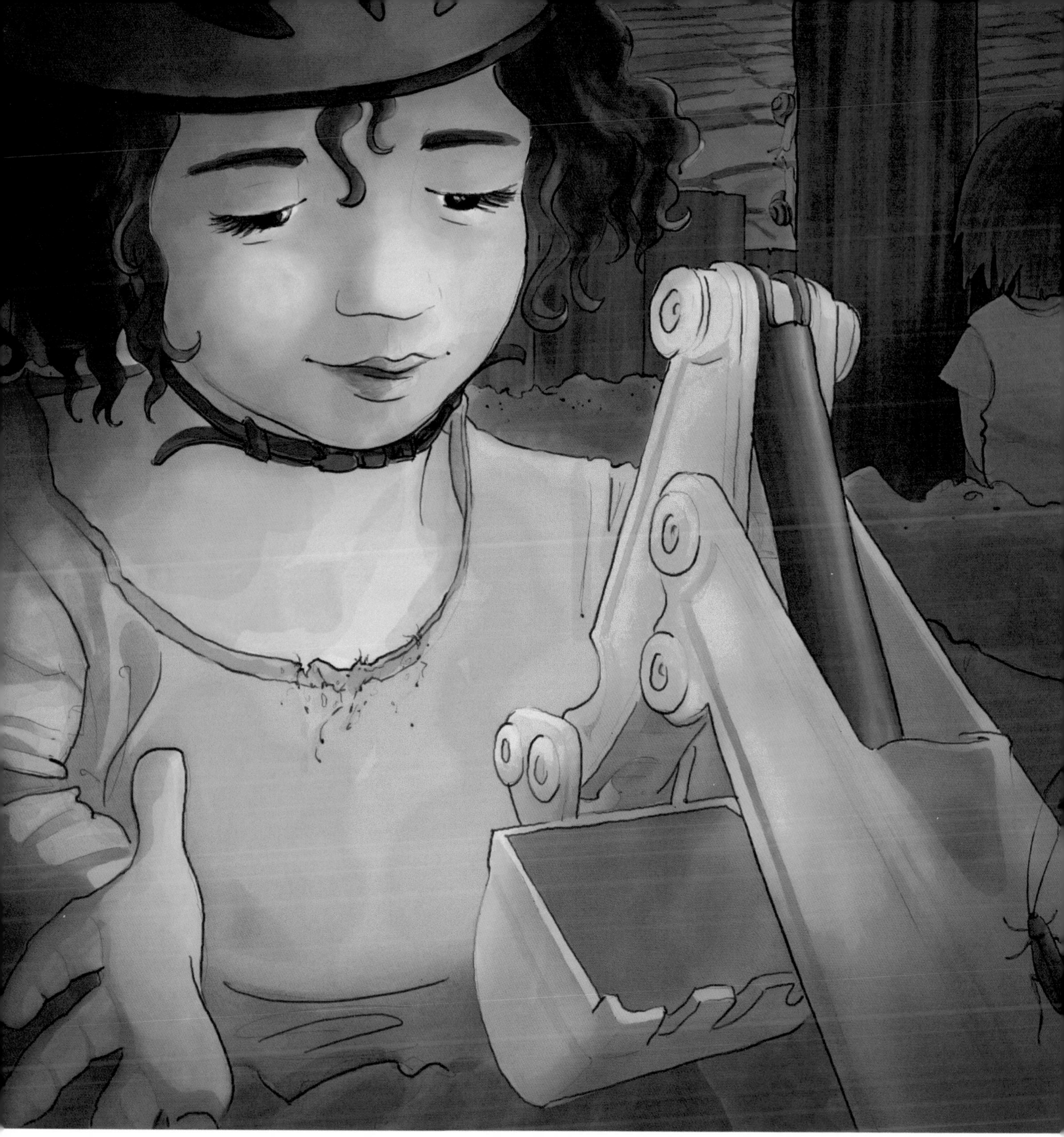

His digger.

tlhanwI'Daj.

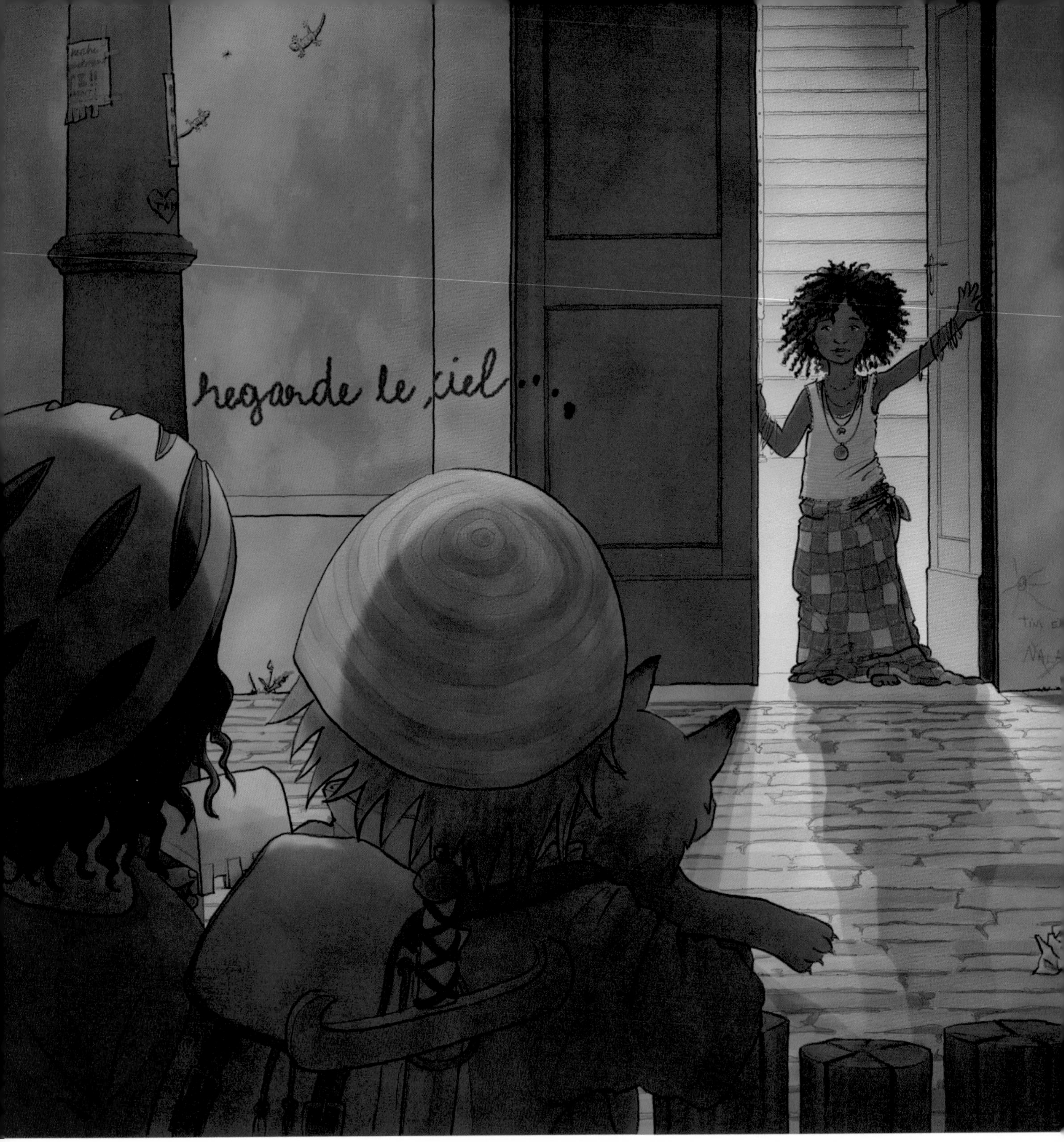
regarde le ciel...

And what is Nala looking for?

'ej nuq nej nala?

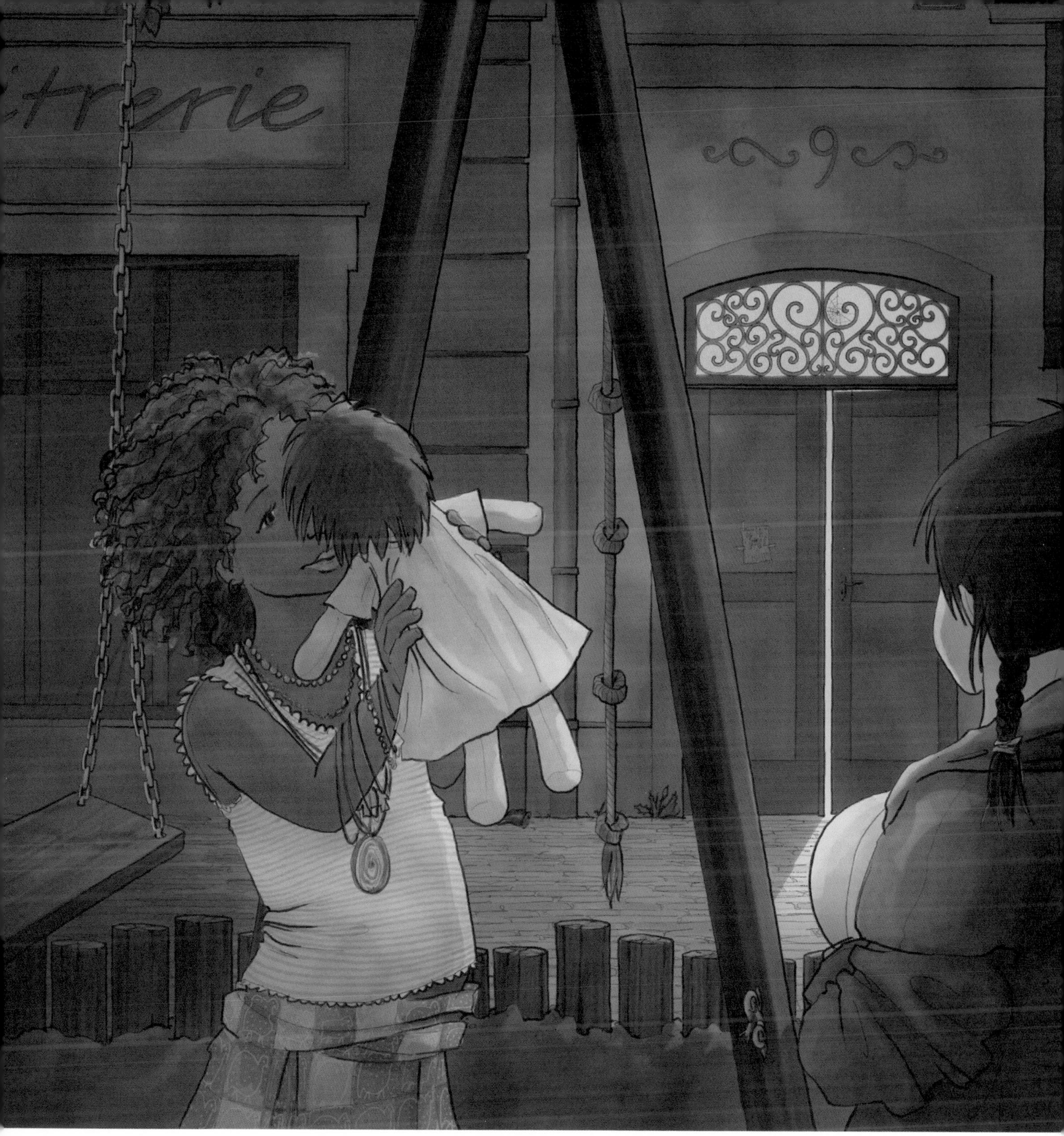

trerie

Her doll.

raghghanDaj.

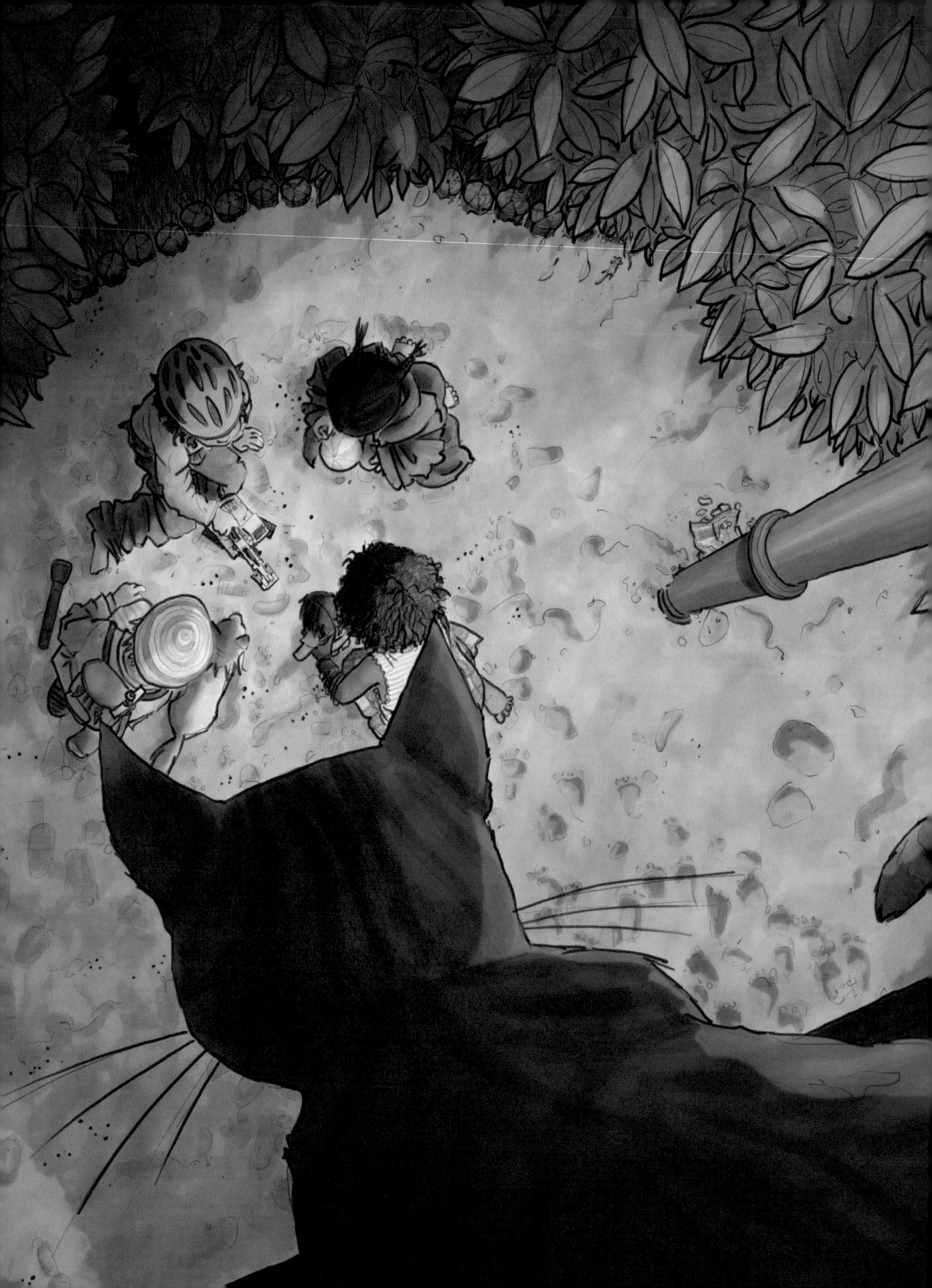

Don't the children have to go to bed?

The cat is rather surprised.

QongDaqDaq ratlh puqpu' net poQbe''a'?

SIvchu' vIghro'.

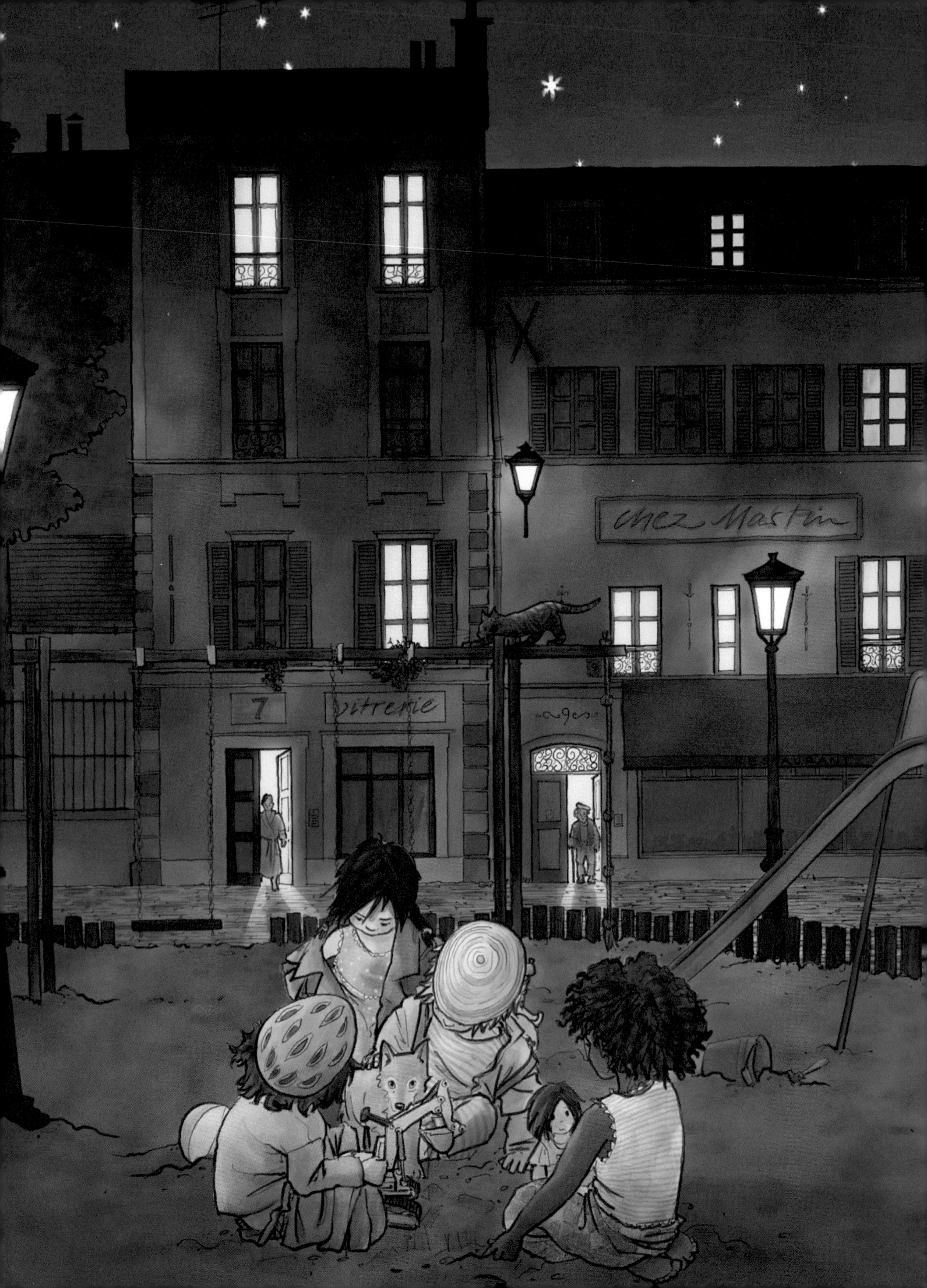

chez Martin
7
vitrerie
9

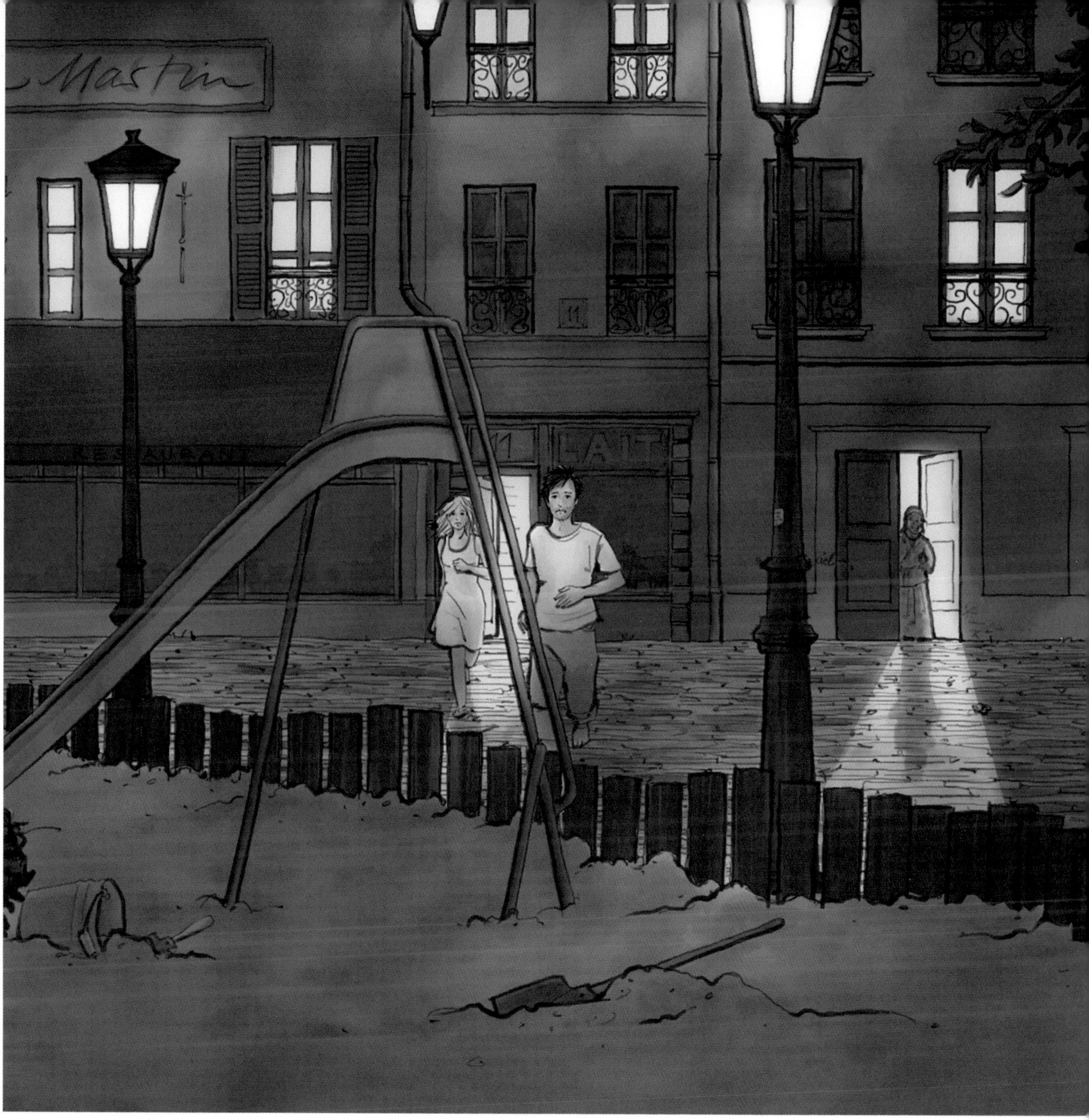
11
LAIT

Who’s coming now?

DaH chol 'Iv?

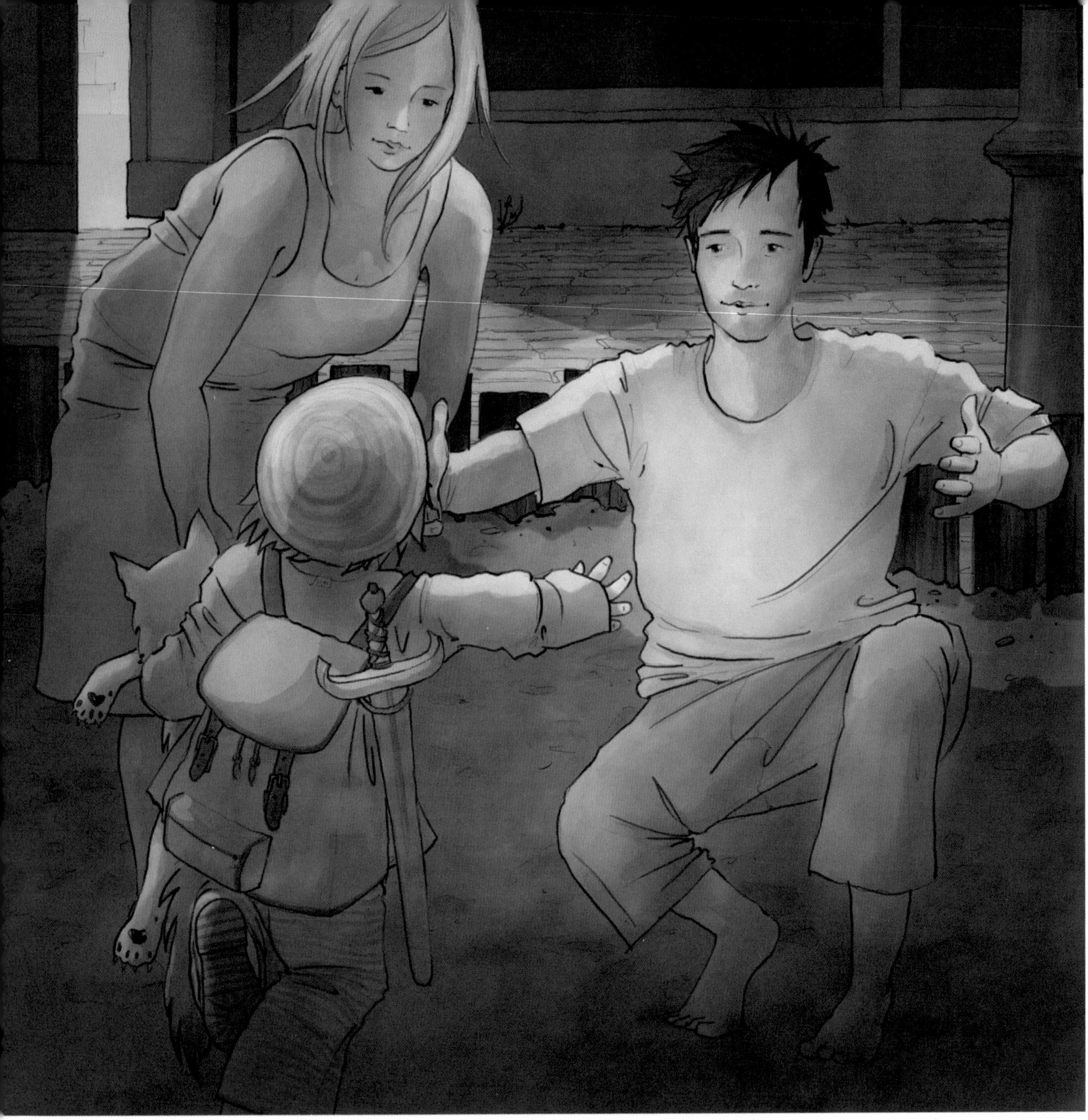

Tim’s mum and dad!

They can’t sleep without their Tim.

chol tIm SoS, tIm vav je!

tImDaj luHutlhtaHvIS QonglaHbe' chaH.

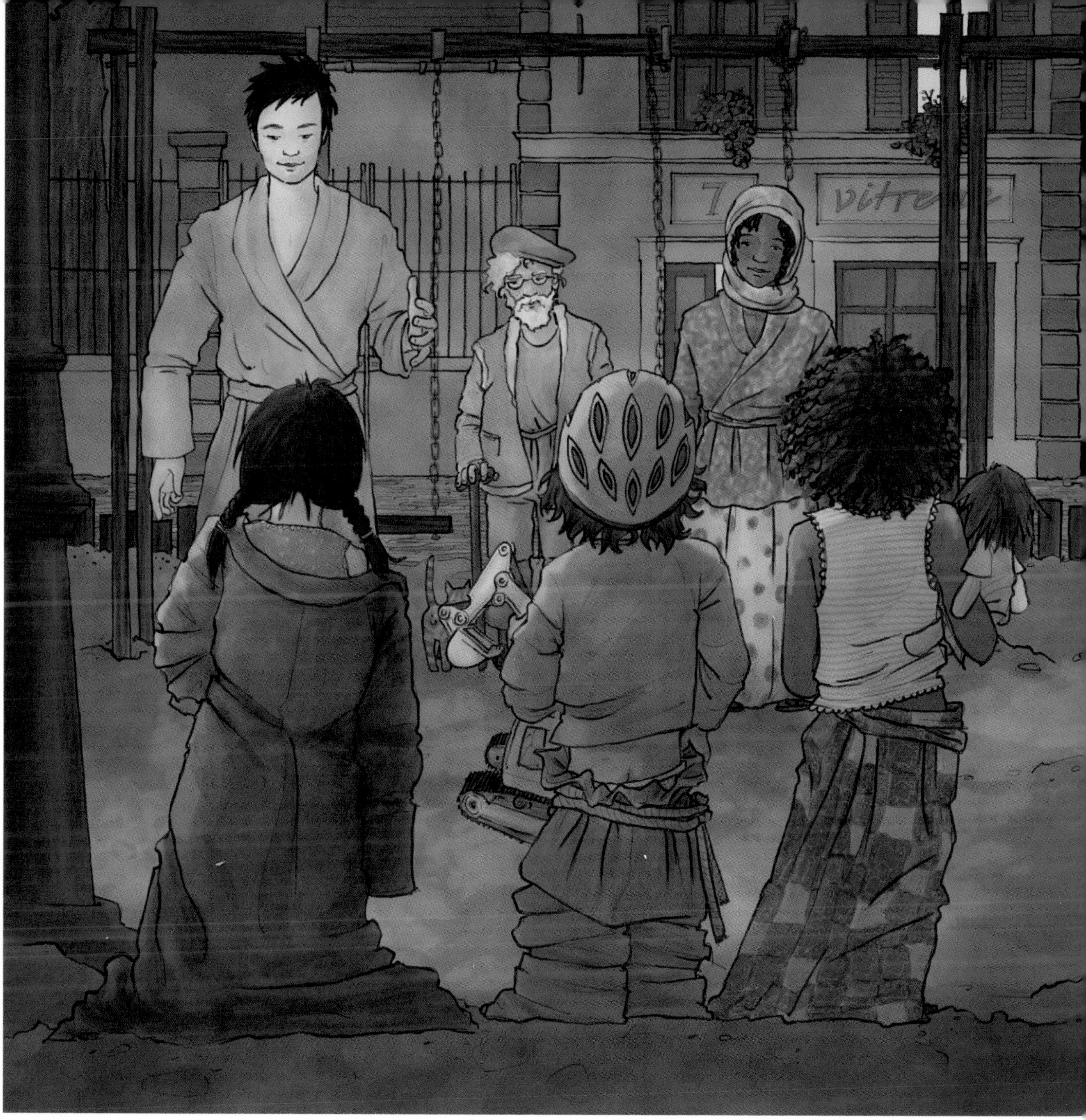

More of them are coming! Marie’s dad.
Tobi’s grandpa. And Nala’s mum.

cholI' latlhpu' law'. marIy vav.
tobIy vavnI'. nala SoS je.

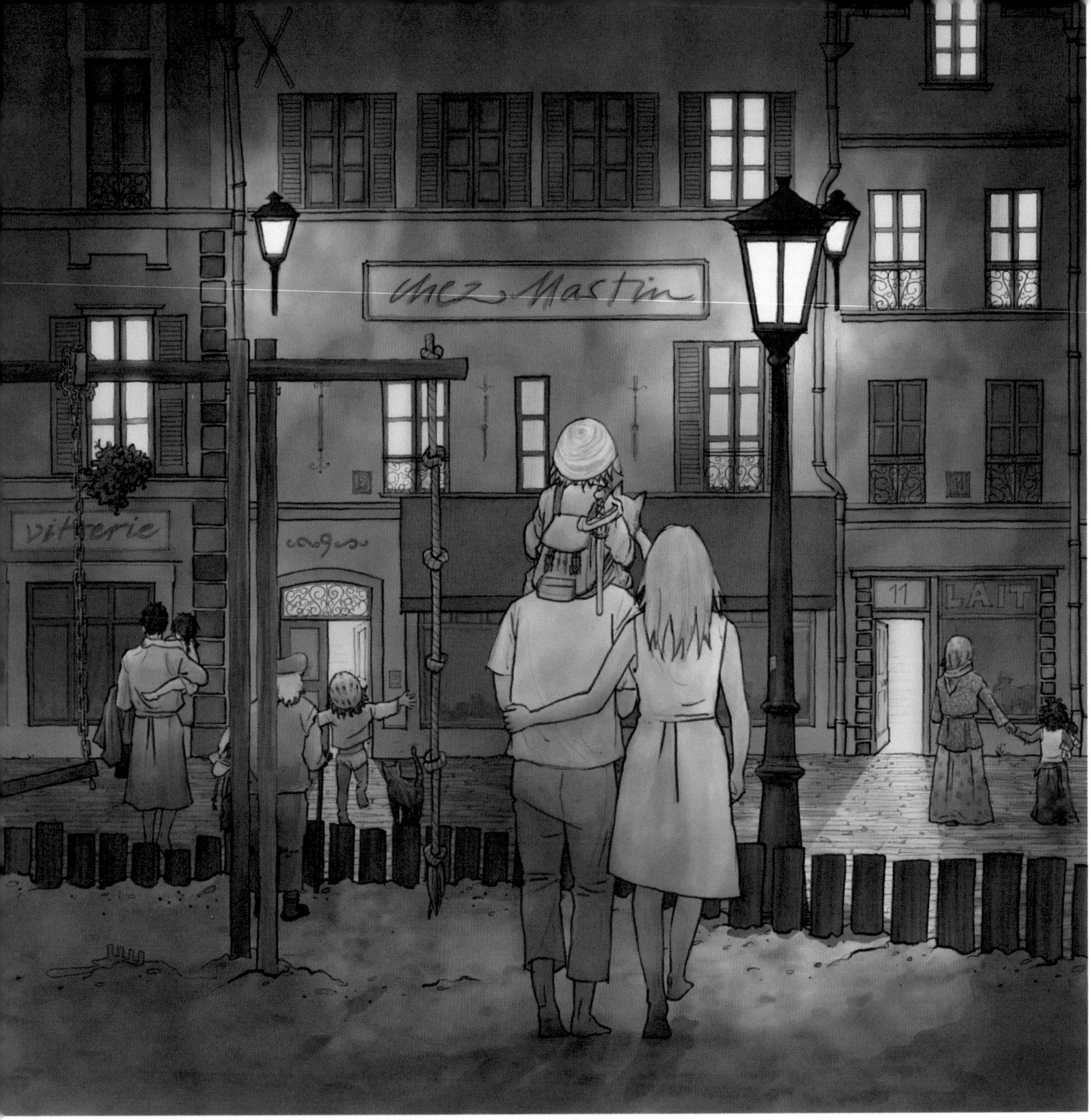
vitrerie
11
LAIT

Now hurry to bed everyone!

QongDaq yIghoS. qul DIr yISop.

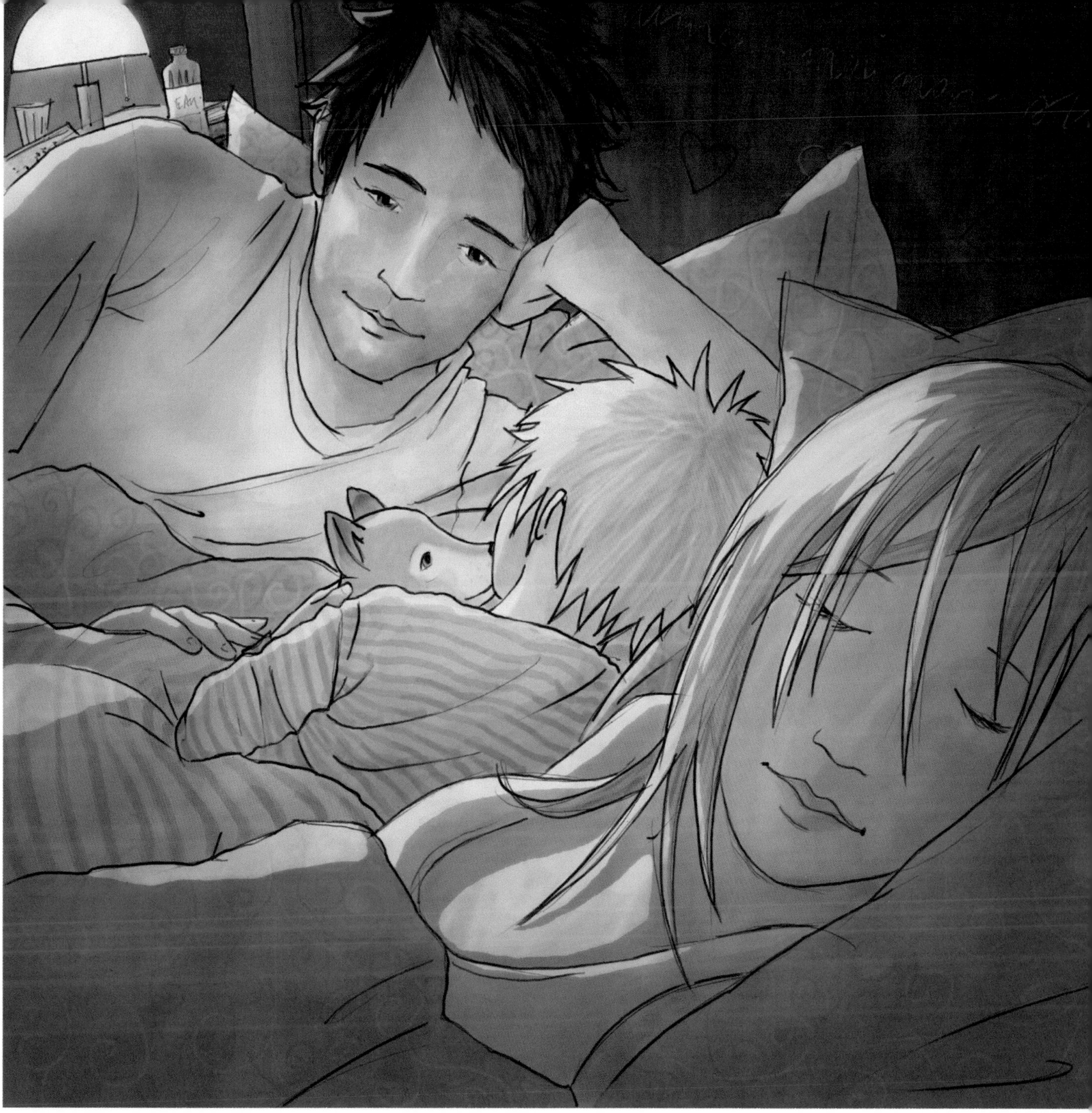

Good night, Tim!

Tomorrow we won’t have to search any longer.

maj ram, tIm!

wa'leS manejnISqa'be'.

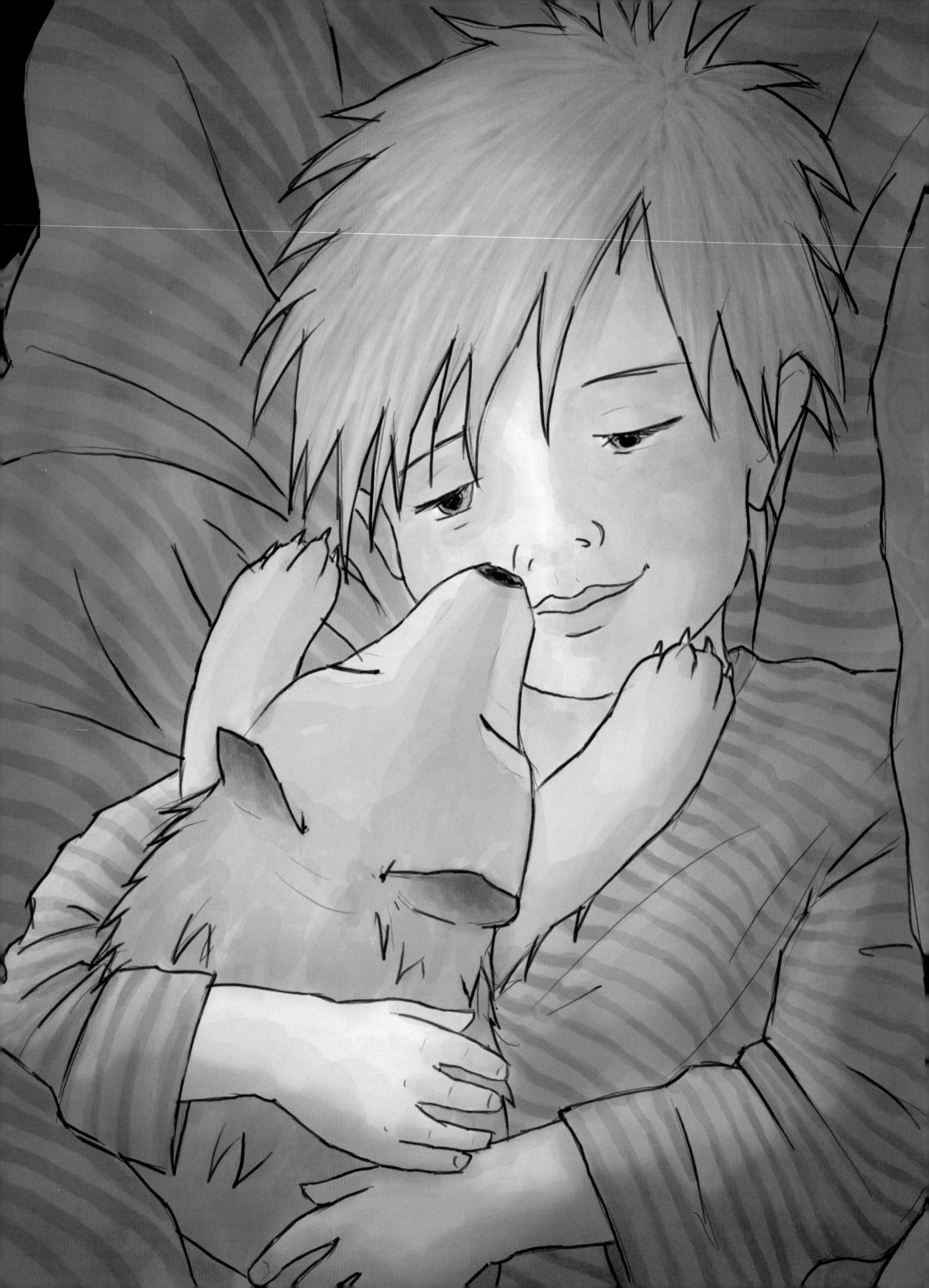

Sleep tight, little wolf!

Qongchu', ngavyaw' mach!

Dear Reader,

Thanks for choosing my book! If you (and most of all, your child) liked it, please spread the word via a Facebook-Like or an email to your friends:

www.sefa-bilingual.com/like

I would also be happy to get a comment or a review. Likes and comments are great TLC for authors, thanks so much!

If there is no audiobook version in your language yet, please be patient! We are working on making all the languages available as audiobooks. You can check the „Language Wizard" for the latest updates:

www.sefa-bilingual.com/languages

Now let me briefly introduce myself: I was born in Stuttgart in 1960, together with my twin brother Herbert (who also became a writer). I studied French literature and a couple of languages in Paris, then medicine in Lübeck. However, my career as a doctor was brief because I soon discovered books: medical books at first, for which I was an editor and a publisher, and later non-fiction and children's books.

I live with my wife Kirsten in Lübeck in the very north of Germany; together we have three (now grown) children, a dog, two cats, and a little publishing house: Sefa Press.

If you want to know more about me, you are welcome to visit my website: **www.ulrichrenz.de**

Best regards,

Ulrich Renz

The illustrator

Barbara Brinkmann was born in Munich in 1969 and grew up in the foothills of the Bavarian Alps. She studied architecture in Munich and is currently a research associate in the Department of Architecture at the Technical University of Munich. She also works as a freelance graphic designer, illustrator, and author.

www.bcbrinkmann.de

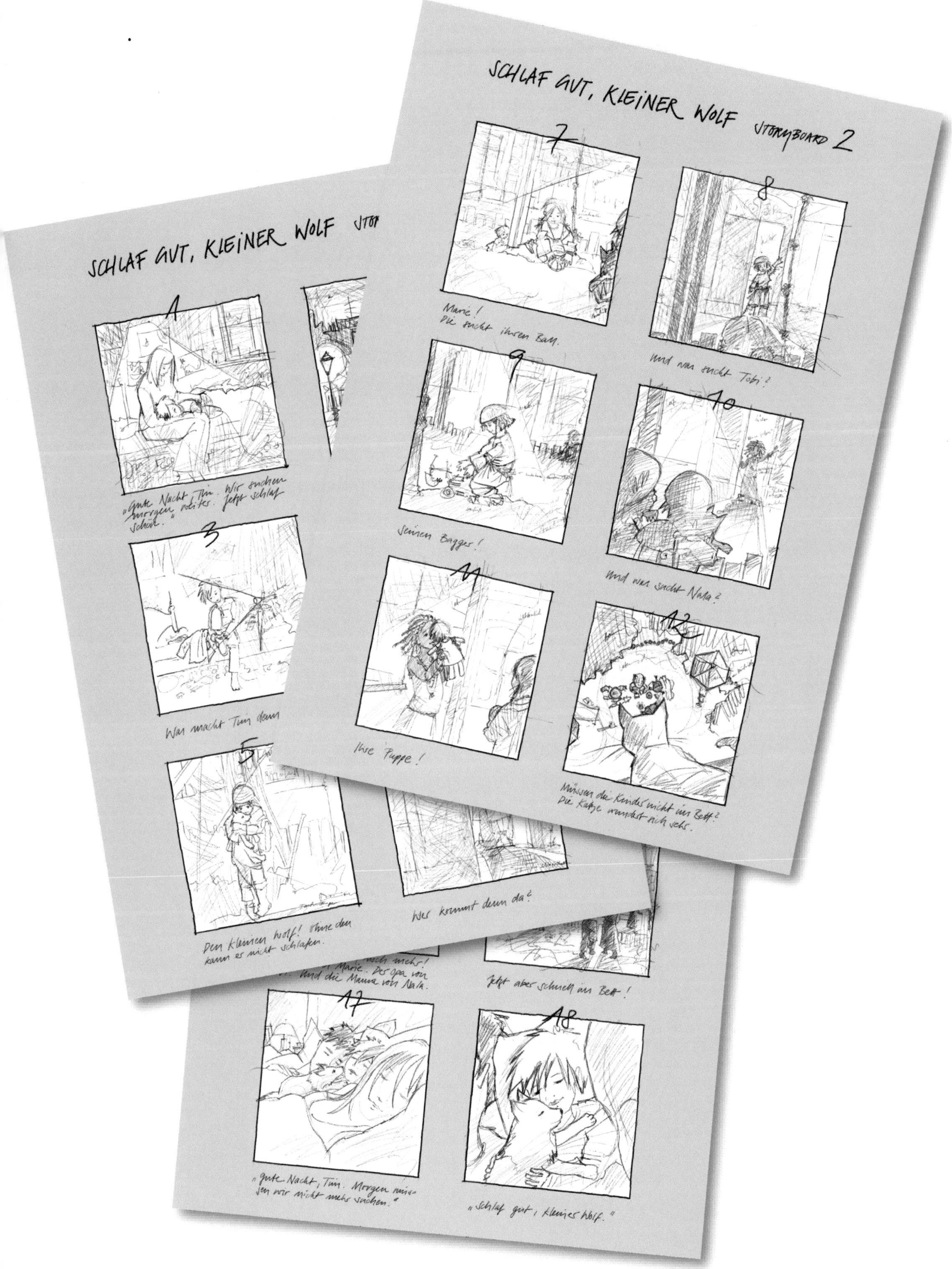
SCHLAF GUT, KLEINER WOLF
SCHLAF GUT, KLEINER WOLF STORYBOARD 2
Marie!
Die sucht ihren Ball.
Und was sucht Tobi?
Seinen Bagger!
Und was sucht Nala?
Ihre Puppe!
Müssen die Kinder nicht ins Bett?
Die Katze wundert sich sehr.
Was macht Tim denn
Den kleinen Wolf! Ohne den kann es nicht schlafen.
Wer kommt denn da?
Und die Mama von Nala.
Jetzt aber schnell ins Bett!
„Gute Nacht, Tim. Morgen müssen wir nicht mehr suchen."
„Schlaf gut, kleiner Wolf."

The Klingon language –
What is that anyway?

Some people will argue that Klingons don't exist – and they are absolutely right. But their language does exist! In the very first cinema adventure of the Star Trek series from 1979, a few syllables were already spoken in Klingon. Some years later, when the grim Klingons returned to the screen, the producers commissioned the linguist Marc Okrand to develop an entire language from the word fragments of the first film. The cornerstone was thus laid and the language slowly began to grow.

With the great success of Star Trek in the nineties the interest for Klingon increased among the fans, so that the language quickly became more than just a film props. Works of world literature have been translated, Klingon operas performed, and even music groups have sung in Klingon.

The reasons for the amazing vitality of the language are certainly manifold. For some, learning Klingon is simply an interesting mental challenge, others enjoy the connection to Star Trek. But the bottom line is that everyone agrees that learning Klingon is fun.

The real fun factor in learning the language is the Klingon seminar in Saarbrücken, which has been held every year since 2002 and attracts participants from all over the world. The so-called qepHom offers the possibility for every student to learn Klingon and to meet like-minded people.

Information about the course and other information:

www.qepHom.de (in German and English)

and

www.klingonisch.com (German)

The Klingon teacher Lieven L. Litaer

© Dennis Eckert / Müncher Science & Fiction Festival

Lieven L. Litaer was born in Belgium in 1980 and now lives in Saarbrücken, Germany. In 1995 he got to know and love Star Trek and began to learn Klingon on his own. He is now one of the world's leading experts in this language. In Germany, he has made himself a reputation especially by his translation into Klingon of the children's book classic "The Little Prince". In 2019 this translation won him the "Deutscher Phantastik Preis".

Since 2002, he has organised an annual language symposium of several days, which has grown into the world's largest Klingon language course and has acquired international popularity.

Litaer regularly gives lectures at conventions, universities and congresses and is involved in numerous translation and voice over projects.

More about Lieven L. Litaer:

www.klingonisch.net

Do you like drawing?

Here are the pictures from the story to color in:

www.sefa-bilingual.com/coloring

Enjoy!

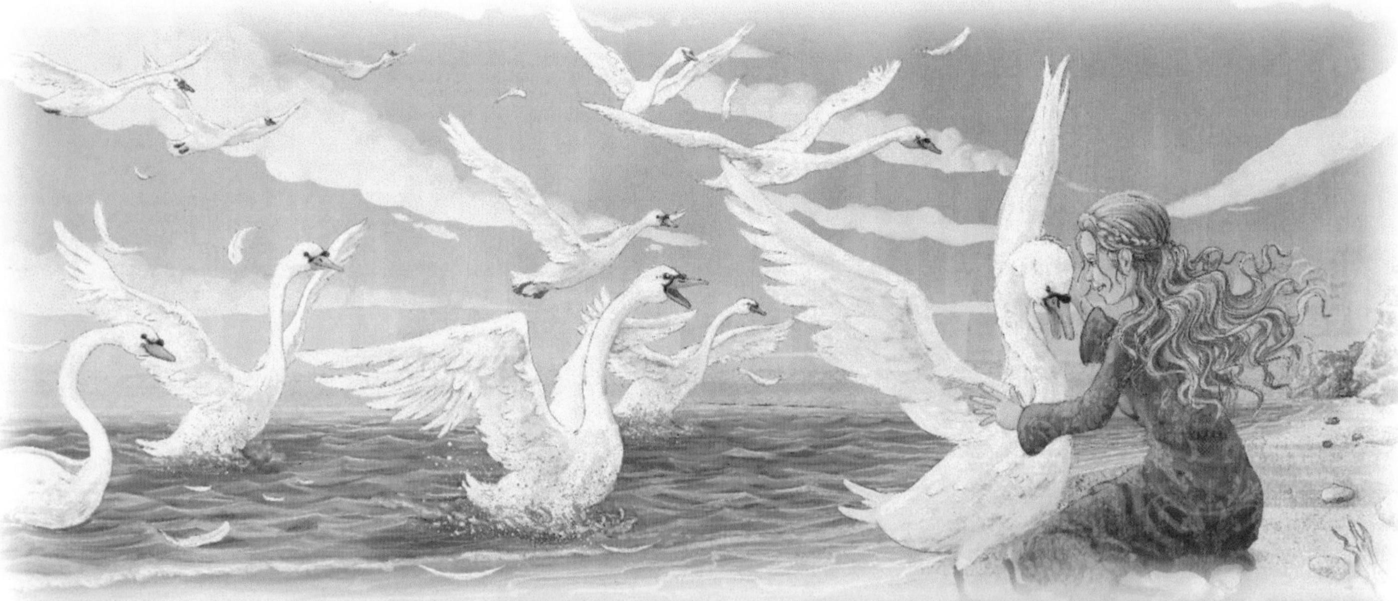

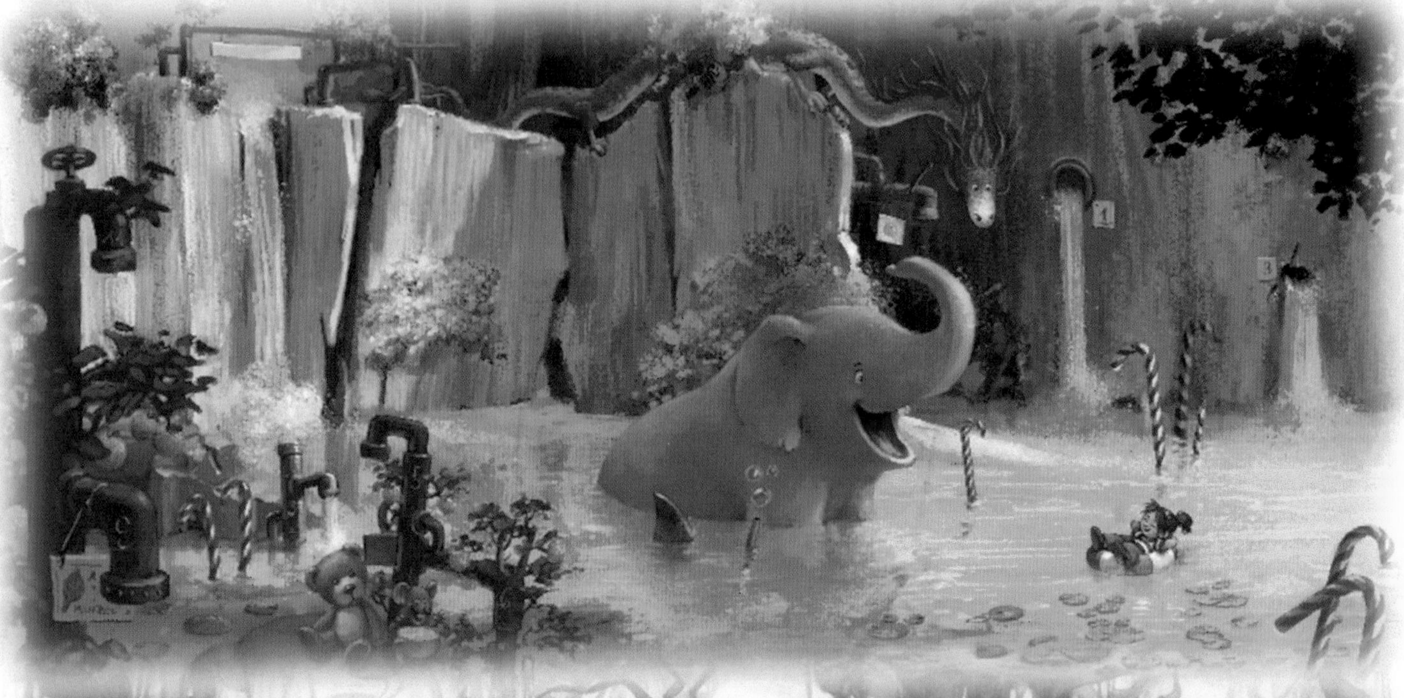

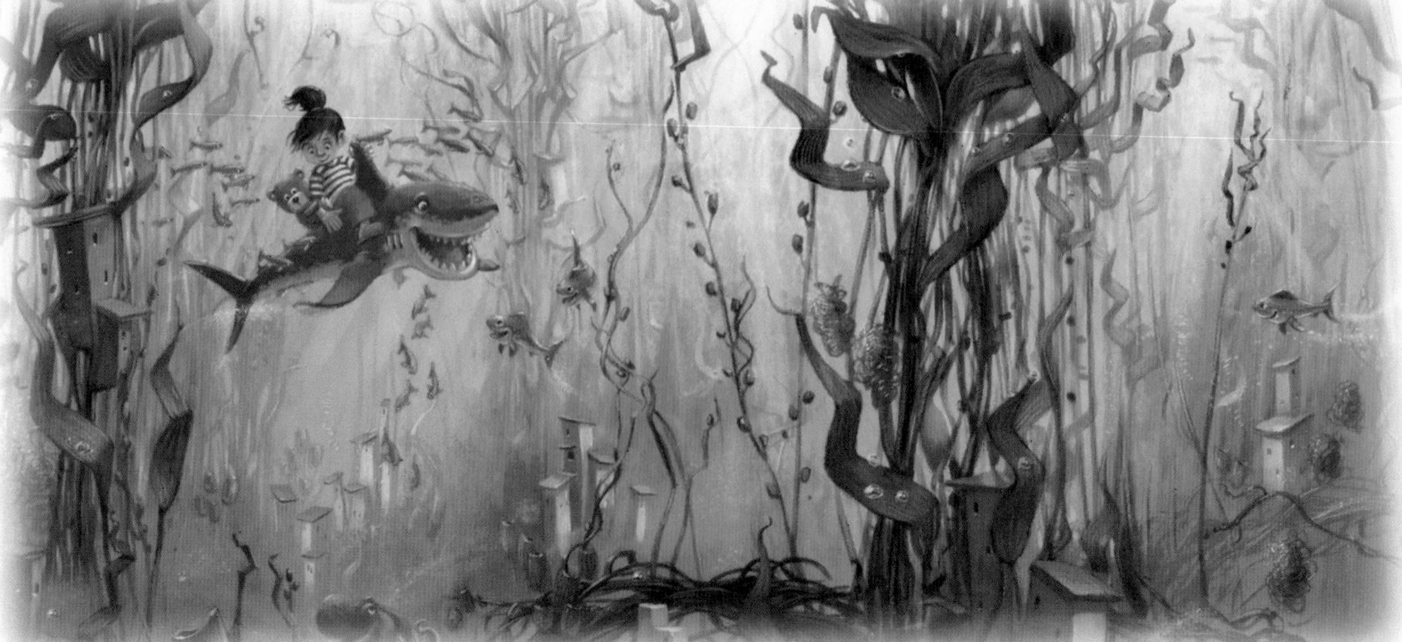

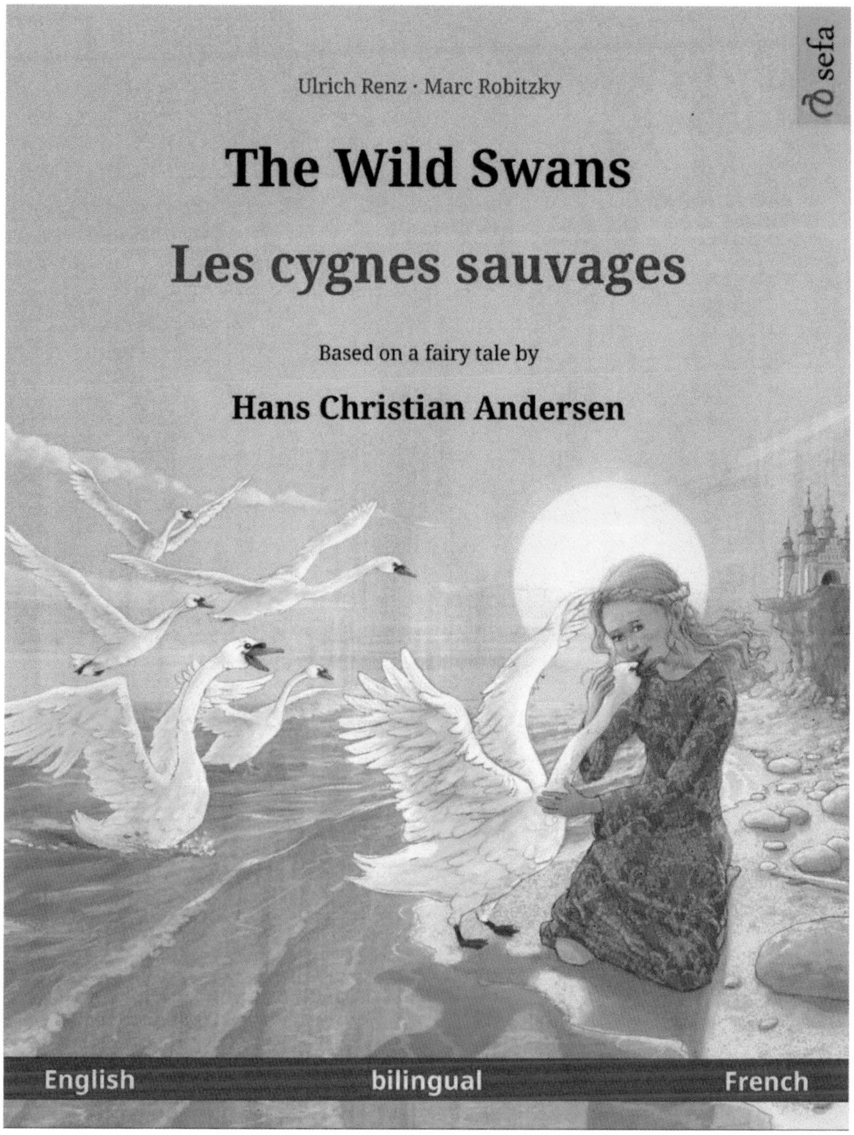
sefa
Ulrich Renz · Marc Robitzky
The Wild Swans
Les cygnes sauvages
Based on a fairy tale by
Hans Christian Andersen
English
bilingual
French

The Wild Swans

Based on a fairy tale by Hans Christian Andersen

► Recommended age: 4-5 and up

„The Wild Swans" by Hans Christian Andersen is, with good reason, one of the world's most popular fairy tales. In its timeless form it addresses the issues out of which human dramas are made: fear, bravery, love, betrayal, separation and reunion.

Available in your languages?

► Check out with our „Language Wizard":

www.sefa-bilingual.com/languages

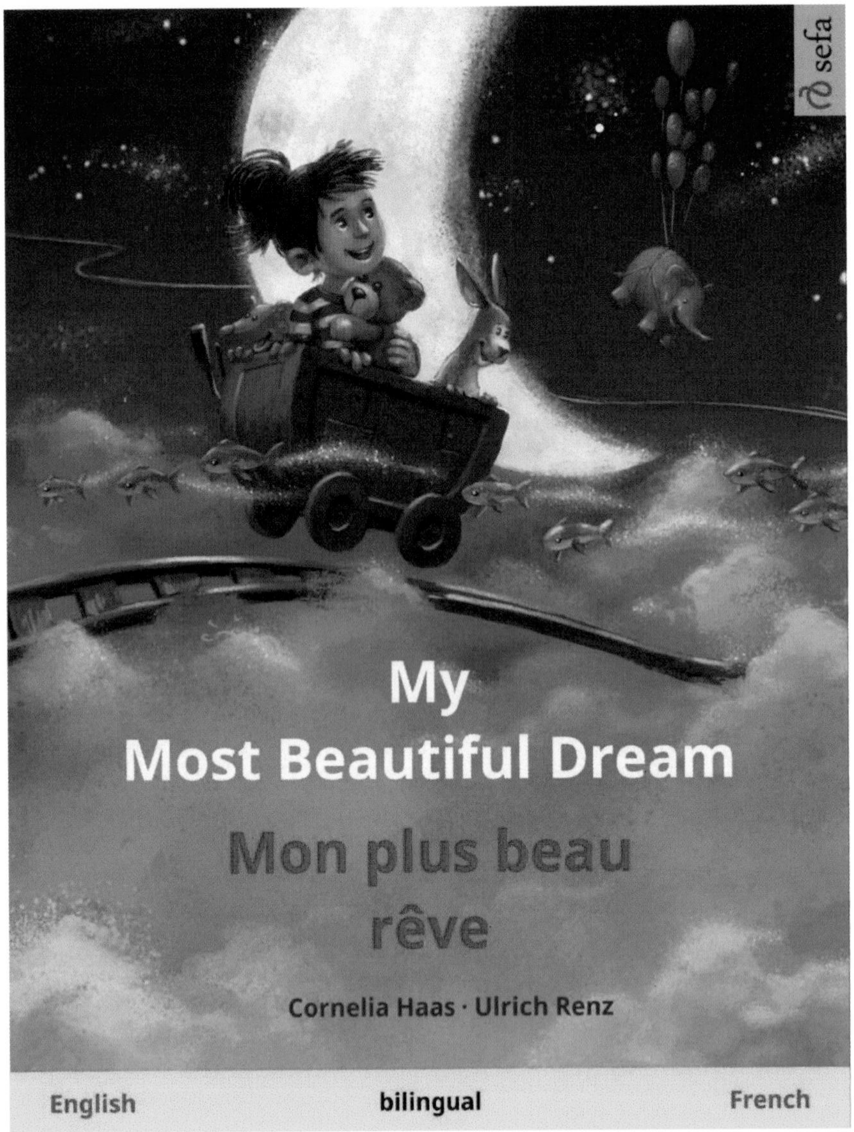
sefa
My
Most Beautiful Dream
Mon plus beau
rêve
Cornelia Haas · Ulrich Renz
English
bilingual
French

My Most Beautiful Dream

► Recommended age: 3-4 and up

Lulu can't fall asleep. All her cuddly toys are dreaming already – the shark, the elephant, the little mouse, the dragon, the kangaroo, and the lion cub. Even the bear has trouble keeping his eyes open ...

Hey bear, will you take me along into your dream?

Thus begins a journey for Lulu that leads her through the dreams of her cuddly toys – and finally to her own most beautiful dream.

Available in your languages?

► Check out with our „Language Wizard":

www.sefa-bilingual.com/languages

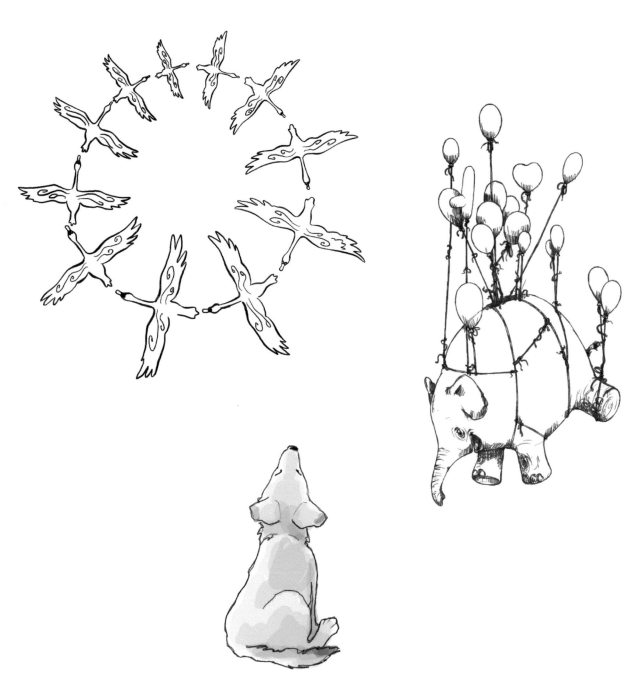

Visit us!

www.sefa-bilingual.com

© 2019 by Sefa Verlag Kirsten Bödeker, Lübeck, Germany

www.sefa-verlag.de

IT: Paul Bödeker, München, Germany

Font: Noto Sans

ISBN: 9783739910697

Version: 20190101

Printed in Great Britain
by Amazon